COMMON or GARDEN COWS

Karen Humpage

Matador
9 Priory Business Park,
Wistow Road, Kibworth Beauchamp,
Leicestershire. LE8 0RX
Tel: 0116 279 2299
Email: books@troubador.co.uk
Web: www.troubador.co.uk/matador
Twitter: @matadorbooks

ISBN 978 1838590 178
British Library Cataloguing in Publication Data.
A catalogue record for this book is available from the British Library.

Printed and bound by CPI Group (UK) Ltd, Croydon, CR0 4YY
Typeset in 11.5pt Giovanni by Troubador Publishing Ltd, Leicester, UK

Matador is an imprint of Troubador Publishing Ltd

For Mum and Dad.

If the celestial library doesn't have it in, maybe they could order you a copy.
Pity we never got the chance to reminisce about the cows together.

Contents

Author's note

In its embryonic stage this book was a simpler, almost picture book affair. It had the paintings on one page with a small amount of narrative text on the opposite page. But that was before I decided to include quotations, and before I started writing stuff around the quotations, and embellishing the text with drawings and photos.

You can still read this book solely by the original text which is now situated underneath the paintings, and it will still form a complete, but simpler, story. Something for parents to read together with their children while studying the pictures.

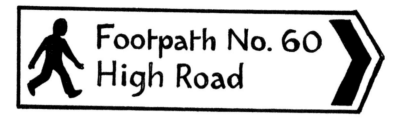

1. How it all began

I'll never forget the look on my boyfriend's face when I opened my front door to greet him one day back in 1980. Ashen-faced and with some reluctance, he informed me that he'd met up with several cows in a nearby alleyway. Being an inhabitant of a land several miles away in the wrong direction, he'd never encountered such a surreal tableau before. Maybe he was afraid of being viewed as some sort of crackpot by his new girlfriend, or of experimenting with the latest *drug du jour*.

"Oh, them," I replied indifferently. "Yes, they're always wandering about the streets."

I don't know if he was more relieved that I had believed him, or crestfallen that I had found such an astonishing occurrence (to him) of no consequence at all.

But that was the way it was back then. Every spring, local residents or 'commoners' with a certain acreage of land and a few cows, were allowed to take their animals onto the 'common land' of Epping Forest and graze their cattle there from April to November. There were no physical boundaries or fences around the commons apart from a few cattle grids of questionable usefulness, so the cows wandered about wherever they wanted to. Occasionally, you'd see a group of cows being moved from one pasture to another by a herdsman, but for the most part they were left to their own devices. So they ended up wandering the streets, which is where my boyfriend came in.

Many years later, my husband (who was the boyfriend back then) was recounting this tale to a neighbour of ours. Not without embellishment, he spun a tale of cows wandering the streets of suburbia for all to see.

"You've got to be joking, mate," was the reply from our neighbour. "What were you on at the time? Got any photos to prove it?"

Well… no, we hadn't. You see, twenty or thirty years ago people didn't take photos with anything like the regularity they do nowadays. With smartphones and digital cameras just a twinkle in some inventor's eye, photography involved complicated rolls of film that had to be taken to the chemist's or sent away to be developed, with a limit of twelve, twenty-four or thirty-six pictures and no preview screen to see if you'd got your subject in the frame or if you'd accidentally taken a picture of your foot. Photography was largely reserved for holidays, days out or weddings.

So, it got me thinking. *Someone* out there must have a picture of a cow in a garden stuffing its face with roses. *Someone* must have had the photographical *nous* to take a picture of a cow without obscuring the lens with a forefinger. Maybe someone on an online forum would be able to help me with my dilemma?

I belong to a few local community groups on Facebook, so I wrote a very simple post: "Does anyone have any photos of a herd of cows walking round the back streets (of Woodford/Wanstead/Epping)?" Responses came in thick and fast as people recounted their memories of the cows. Cows in gardens. Cows in shops. Cows in the middle of the road. Cows on roundabouts. Cows in playgrounds. Seems cows got just about everywhere.

Sadly, the photos were not quite so forthcoming. As I suspected, people didn't snap things with quite the same earnestness as they do these days. Photographic diarrhoea wasn't a new and strange affliction that perversely bunged up your computer with thousands and thousands of uncategorised and untitled selfies and photographs of what you had for dinner. But then maybe there were lots of old photographs of feet and thumbs mouldering away in dog-eared envelopes at the bottom of wardrobes.

" …[cows] were just so common in the '70s and '80s that none of us would bother to take a photo. Would've been like photographing ducks on a pond. "

Bored one evening, I started scribbling cows in my sketchbook. If photographs were thin on the ground, maybe I could bring some of the anecdotes to life in pencil and paint?

And so started a year-long obsession with painting cows. I shortlisted anecdotes that I felt would paint a good picture and sketched scenarios to bring them to life. Most of the paintings are based on responses received from locals, so could be technically classed as factually based, though some might have had the boundaries of credulity stretched a little bit. But flying kites on Chingford Plain *was* a popular childhood pastime, and there *were* cows on the plain…

The photographs eventually started to trickle in – and confirmed to our neighbour once and for all that we hadn't been glue sniffing.

AT THE WATERING HOLE – HOLLOW PONDS

On the outskirts of London, there is a big forest called Epping Forest. It is a very old forest, where deer and rabbits and badgers live. Owls, robins and lots of other birds live in the canopy of the mighty oak and beech trees, and little fishes and frogs live in the ponds and lakes.

Scattered through the big forest are towns and villages where people live. When they are not at school or work, people like to go into the forest, as it is a nice place to play and walk. Families go there to kick a ball about, to walk the dog or to have a picnic. Not so long ago, farmers took their cattle to the forest to eat the grass. There were lots of fields for the cows to roam about in, and trees and bushes to shelter under when it was raining.

Sometimes the cows came out of the forest and came into contact with people as they went about their daily lives.

2. Gardens

One of the joys of my Facebook request was reading the wealth of anecdotes I received from people who remembered the cows. Most people had memories of cows in front gardens, chewing their way through hedges, summer bedding and rosebushes. Everybody mentioned rosebushes (well, not quite everyone). I was beginning to think it was just a lazy phrase that people trotted out about 'cows eating all the roses', until the photographs started coming in of cows in front gardens with… rosebushes. Particularly hybrid teas. Our own front garden had a sprawling, dark red bush of unknown parentage with a heady fragrance, and a 'Piccadilly' rose – yellow with red-rimmed petals – which I loved as a child. Fortunately, they were in a part of the garden that was difficult for the cows to reach, so they had to content themselves by making an enormous hole in the privet hedge.

Being social animals, the cows liked to travel about in groups. Which made a visitation all the more worrisome, as the potential for disaster was so much greater. There wasn't much you could do if four or five cows chose to eat your particular roses, apart from shout at them from the safety of your front doorstep. Waving a tea towel vigorously at them was a popular choice, though a red one may not have been a good idea. Alternatively, banging a metal tea tray or blowing an old car horn at them worked for people faint of voice. Brooms and umbrellas seemed to be the choice weapon of attack when trying to remove cows from gardens, but then I suppose people grabbed the nearest thing to hand. Even a handful of old Ever Readies were used as missiles, opportunistically plucked from the pocket of a housewife's tabard, as she was changing the batteries in her radio at the time.

COWS IN MY FRONT GARDEN

Sometimes cows wandered around the streets and houses where people lived.
The cows liked to eat all the pretty flowers growing in people's gardens. They chomped
on the red roses. They chewed on the big yellow sunflowers. They trod on the pink
geraniums. As a 'thank you' they left little packages behind on the pathway for people
to tread in.

> " ...they used to sound like a group of girls wearing heels walking up the road. If we didn't shut our gate properly [Hartley Road], they'd crowd into our little front garden eating the flowers and we'd be trapped inside the house until they moved on. "

It seemed cows instinctively knew that a ratio of four cows to two humans would enable at least some of them to get a chance to eat a few tasty blooms. A couple of cows would keep the humans occupied by getting them to chase them, while their accomplices would raid the garden. Those cows would get their turn in the next garden when another two cows would engage the humans in a game of tag.

> " The cows who plagued us in the '50s and '60s... were quite fearless of humans, and sometimes aggressive if they had happened to have got out of their stall on the wrong side. On one visit - after I had spent some weeks creating my front lawn from scratch, building up a fine tilth of a foot or more of laboriously-sieved soil, sown the finest grass seed and was rewarded with a crop of billiard table-like green sward - along came a dozen of the bovine bulldozers and not only cropped the gourmet-standard grass, but left the lawn honeycombed with deep holes. At the same time, they set about the flower garden of my neighbour opposite, and munched their way through his daffodils, roses and crocuses. By the time we had got on the scene, the devastation was just about complete, and the language of us all was unprintable. "

MAYHEM IN MONKHAMS

The houses on the edge of Knighton Wood had big gardens with carefully tended lawns.

Cows liked to visit these gardens because there were lots of tasty flowers to eat.

The cows barged through the low hedges to get at the flowerbeds, where they greedily tucked into the roses and the daffodils.

Mrs Stevens ran out of the house waving her broom in the air when she saw the cows coming.

Mr Mason the gardener set about the cows with his hose, spraying water everywhere.

Patch the dog, from two doors down, thought this was all part of an exciting game and ran to join in the fun.

One cow found something interesting to look at through the windows of the caravan.

I wonder what he saw?

Even the law wasn't immune from a raid by cows. Wanstead Police Station once boasted a beautifully manicured garden tended by one of the officers, which won an award for 'best garden' back in the '70s. However, the night before the award was presented to the proud gardener, the cows moved in and ate much of the display.

Not everyone was bothered though when the cows came to town. Some people liked the cows eating the grass in their gardens, as it saved them a job mowing it. Constant supervision was required though to keep the cows from sneak-eating all the yummy flowers.

Unfortunately, cows disappeared from front gardens at around the same time gardens became entombed in concrete. Very different beasts moved in, as members of the one-car family shouted, "Me too!" and wanted their own personal gas-guzzling tin chariot to bung up the roads with.

Give me a bus and a bed of snapdragons any day!

MOW COW

Some people didn't mind it when the cows came to town. Mr Fosdyke liked it when they came and trimmed his lawn and hedges, as it gave him a chance to catch up with some important reading.

3. Traffic

A commuter's day would not start well if they opened their front door to find a cow or three standing in the front garden. Having to run the gauntlet past a large cow to the gate was not an exercise most people would relish unless they fancied their self as a contestant on *It's a Knockout*. So most people waited until the cows moved on, leading to many seemingly outlandish excuses as to why they were late for work.

> " I remember the cows well. we used to live in Beverley Crescent and I once had to call work to say I'd be late, as three cows were in our front garden and I couldn't get out of the house. They thought I was mad! "

The daily drudgery of waiting for a bus could be alleviated by the spectacle of a cow joining the commute. Not privy to the tradition of queuing, a cow could fill a whole bus shelter, leaving the poor commuters resigned to standing out in the inevitable rain.

> " There was a wooden bus shelter on Lake House road... in it waiting for a bus was an enormous cow just standing there minding its own business. "

It didn't stop there. An old friend of mine had this fair tale to tell:

COWMAGEDDON

Mayhem ensued one day when a herd of cows stopped the traffic in the High Street.
Mrs Mountjoy got a shock when a cow peered into the back of her car. Susie the shop
assistant fell off her bicycle and spilled sticky buns all over the pavement. Mr Tibbins
the greengrocer tried to wave away the cows with his leeks. Mr Snodgrass the bank
manager tried to shoo a cow off his car with a rolled-up newspaper. All the while, the
passengers on the bus watched in amusement at the drama below them.

I was a student at the South West Essex Technical College and School of Art during the early '60s. On one particular morning I had to catch the 123 bus from Waterworks Corner on the Woodford New Road to get to college, a short walk which entailed crossing the road by the traffic lights at Waterworks Corner. At that time there was still common grazing rights in Epping Forest and the roundabout was protected from wandering cows by a complex system of self-closing gates and cattle grids.

However, on this day the wooden gate opposite the waterworks was broken. I was waiting for the green man on the lights to appear to let me cross when a cow appeared out of the woods and calmly stood next to me at the crossing. The obedient animal waited until the green man appeared, which allowed the cow and I to cross the road, me going on to the bus stop, bovine turning to the left to continue along the pavement towards St Peter-in-the-Forest and, I assume, the Whipps Cross roundabout. The animal was quite calm about it all. No doubt it was her usual daily promenade. "

If you managed to get as far as the train station, you could be stopped in your tracks by a herd of cows using the subway. South Woodford and Woodford Green stations have long, sloping subways going underneath the underground (Central) line, connecting the north and south parts of George Lane and Snakes Lane respectively. You could get to the bottom of either subway, turn a corner to traverse the uphill slope and find a group of cows coming from the other direction. The choice was yours as to whether to sidle past the cows in the hope they didn't squash you against the wall or go back the way you came.

AN ENCOUNTER AT THE CROSSING

Julian the art student got a surprise one morning when a cow joined him in waiting for the lights to change at the zebra crossing.

On the roads, cows were a constant headache during the grazing season, as they ambled slowly along the main thoroughfares in search of pasture. Often they would just stop, or wander about in the middle of the road as if they weren't sure which direction to go in. They might even lie down on the road if the tarmac was particularly warm, oblivious to cars, buses, lorries and shaking fists.

Roundabouts crop up frequently in people's comments about cows and traffic; quite why cows liked sitting on a roundabout has never been ascertained. Maybe they enjoyed all the attention it afforded them.

66 For many years, cows were a regular feature at the Whipps Cross and the waterworks roundabouts, despite the cattle grids set into the roads! In the summer they would just be lying on the Whipps Cross central reservation chewing grass and gazing at the traffic in an accommodating sort of way. 99

A colourful insight into the day-to-day management of the cattle comes from Christine Brassey, the first female mounted forest keeper who worked in Epping Forest:

66 ...there were quite a few local farmers who had grazing rights on the forest who would turn out their cows in the spring. The cows were usually heifers [young females] and would be allowed to roam and graze freely. The farmers had their own brand to identify their cattle and every year the farmers and Forest Keepers would herd the cattle down to Wanstead Flats for marking. Marking was done by the Reeve [a person responsible for estate management and the branding of cattle]. Herding the cattle was great fun back then, using the horses and motorbikes. Sometimes we would herd them all the way from the Loughton area of Fairmead down to Wanstead. They would duck and dive into the undergrowth and we would have to push them back onto the bridle paths and keep them moving. Driving them across the Green Man roundabout [at Leytonstone] back then was chaos. We brought the traffic to a standstill for a short while, as there was no underpass from Leyton Flats to Bush Wood back then. And on numerous occasions we Forest Keepers had to chase them out of people's gardens and herd them back to the forest. 99

SUBWAY SURPRISE

Cows soon got used to life about town and made full use of the public amenities. Sometimes cows used the subways to get from one place to another. They mastered the art of walking up and down slopes, though they generally avoided using the steps.

With herds of cattle roaming the forest and increasing traffic on the roads through the '60s and '70s, this led to many accidents:

" Sometime in 1968, I was riding my police 'noddy' bike when I got a call to the middle of Wanstead Flats. There I met a farmer and a vet who pointed out a heifer with a bad wound in its side. Apparently it had been hit by a lorry and the farmer and vet had tried in vain to get near enough to put a tranquilizer dart in the animal so that it could be taken away for treatment. The vet showed me a large tubular dart and asked me to have go on my motorbike. I accepted the challenge and advanced slowly and, because the velocette bike was water-cooled, almost silently. Well, after a couple of failed attempts, I decided to approach from the back of the animal at speed, then cut the engine and hope. I felt like a cross between characters in two films, *Electraglide in Blue* and *Rawhide*. Anyway, it worked, and I stuck the dart into the animal, after which

it quickly went to sleep and was taken away for treatment.

Two days later, I met the farmer at the Duke of Wellington at High Beech for a 'thank you' drink. I've often wondered about the issues that would arise if asked to do the same task today!!! "

A HULLABALOO IN LOUGHTON

Chaos occurred one morning when some cows wandered onto the High Road. Bert the milkman had to swerve suddenly when he nearly drove into a cow, causing all his milk bottles to fall off the back of his milk float. Mrs Whitworth brandished a French stick to shoo away a startled cow, little realising that another cow was just about to steal her rhubarb. But little six-year-old Herbert just wanted to get out of the car and make friends with the cows.

4. Cowpats and kids

Cow dung, cowpats, cow pies, meadow muffins – whatever you want to call them – cows are very messy beasts. All those masticated hedges, choice bedding plants and prize roses have to vacate their predator at some point, and the resulting porridge is a dark greeny-brown slurry delivered unceremoniously onto the ground, often right in the middle of a pavement. Fresh pats were always the worst, and many a hapless pedestrian has walked straight into one of these, rendering all manner of hosiery and footwear unwearable:

> **"** I remember stepping in a cowpat in my lovely red espadrilles in the church grounds of Holy Trinity on Hermon Hill. **"**

Even worse would be to fall headlong into a cowpat. It was a common recreational hazard amongst rugby and football players on Wanstead Flats, but the occasional unfortunate soul might come across something unmentionable while walking through the long grass.

MOONLIGHT ENCOUNTER

Kevin got a bit of a fright one night returning home from a rock concert. Taking a short cut across the green, he tripped over a slumbering cow hidden in the long grass. Thankfully he had a soft landing.

Not everyone was cross when the cows pooed on the pavement. Gardeners and allotmenteers could benefit from collecting fresh pats for fertilising their flowers and vegetables. Being hardy sorts, most were unabashed to be seen scooping poop off the pavement and into a bucket, though you can bet there were a few furtive night-time collections by those who didn't want to be seen by the neighbours.

Dogs too took great delight in finding a cowpat to sniff at or worse, roll about in. Jack Russells in particular seem to be privy to this doggy peculiarity, much to the disgust of their owners who had to clear up the resulting mess before said pet was allowed back into the home.

Sport would often be made of cowpats, especially by children who would play hopscotch over them, or the more studious could practice their mathematics by counting them. If the pats had dried out in the summer sun, a game of frisbee could be had by those who dared. It was not unusual to see cowpats with twigs sticking in them, or pens and pencils if on a school route.

Bonfire night provided an annual opportunity for boisterous young boys to get up to some monkey business. Banger fireworks were available back then that were intended to be lit and then thrown, where they would explode after a few seconds with a loud bang. An inevitable progression from twigs and pencils would be a banger squished into a cowpat where it would explode, showering cow dung in all directions, often right into the face of their unlucky counterparts.

PATS FOR PARSNIPS

Mr Greengage, an elderly gentleman who owned an allotment, went around collecting
cowpats in a bucket to put on his vegetables. Cow poo makes good fertilizer for plants
and saved Mr Greengage some money as he didn't have to buy any.

Twentieth-century kids spent a great deal of their recreation time outdoors. Gathering in small groups on a street corner or in a park was their social media, and inventing games to play sparked their imagination, creativity and mischief. Consequently, they were a relatively tough bunch, and a herd of cows wandering down the road was an opportunity for fun and not something to run away from, though they did have a healthy respect for the cows' horns. Cattle herding, either on foot or on a bicycle – a Chopper if you were lucky – featured in many anecdotes of people who imagined themselves as cowboys and cowgirls. The Green at Woodford certainly played its part – in summertime, the long grass turned a golden yellow and swayed in the warm breeze and for a little while, one could imagine yourself traversing a vast wild west prairie. One resident summed this up beautifully:

" I grew up in a cul-de-sac in Woodford. At that time there were a crowd of us kids around the same age who played together and would be sent out, by our parents, to shoo the cows out of the road before they ruined the gardens. Our imaginary games of being cowboys came in handy as we whooped and hollered and chased them up to Woodford Green by The Castle. I doubt that the cricket club enjoyed our energetic efforts, but the cows moved happily enough. "

A few anecdotes mention children getting up onto the backs of cows and riding them around. How true this really is I will never be sure, though it is distinctly possible. It seems unbelievable nowadays, but like I said, kids back then were a hardy bunch. Not that I'd recommend it now, though.

" There was one particular cow that would come around every year for about five years and plot up in the 'The Roses' for the whole summer. She was very friendly and didn't mind us kids jumping on her back for a ride. "

PANDEMONIUM IN THE PLAYGROUND

Sometimes cows got into the playground, which would be very exciting for bored schoolchildren. They would rush to the classroom windows to see the cows chasing their friends around the playground. Miss Tufty the PE teacher would blow her whistle furiously at them until she was red in the face.

Cows were very good at alleviating the tedium of the school day. A cow spied from the window of a classroom by a bored pupil would soon become the focus of all of his or her classmates. Desks and chairs would be toppled by pupils in a frenzy to reach the window, leaving the teacher to ineffectively shout for calmness amidst an ever-growing crescendo of excited screams and shrieks. Sometimes cows would find their way into the school grounds (security back then wasn't as tight as it is nowadays). This would escalate the level of excitement to bursting point and the poor teacher would have to concede defeat. And if, on the odd occasion, cows ventured into the grounds at playtime, excitement would be elevated to a stratospheric level. Frightened or fearless, kids would be running in all directions. One resident remembers cows chasing children around the playground at Woodford Green Preparatory School.

Finally I must give a mention to Cow Pie Bingo. Pity children weren't privy to this rural American game at the time, as I'm sure they would have adapted it in some way. A small paddock has grid lines drawn onto the ground and each box created is then numbered. People draw lots or bet on a number. Cows are unleashed into the paddock and the person with the first box that receives a dollop of cow poop is the winner.

EXOTIC PETS

"I miss those cows. I was brought up with them and looked forward to April when the cows would come to town. When the end of September used to arrive, I often wondered how many cows I could get into my flat to save them. Alas, this never happened."

How many cows has this little girl managed to squeeze into her bedroom?

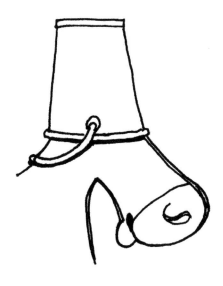

5. Inquisitiveness

Cows are naturally inquisitive beasts. Some are actually quite intelligent. When their wanderings took them outside their natural habitat of the forest and pasture, they were keen to explore the new sights and sounds of suburbia, and especially the new smells and tastes.

Shopkeepers with displays outside their establishments had to be mindful when cows were in the area. A stack of plastic buckets could be easily trodden in or a collection of brooms tipped over. Cows can appear quite clumsy, though they're not really. They're just not used to small spaces and rickety table displays outside shops.

Many a florists' display has been decimated by hungry cows eager to get to the flowers, which must have stood out like brightly coloured sweets in a sea of concrete. And greengrocers had to either cover their wares with a tarpaulin or co-opt neighbouring shopkeepers to create a hullaballoo outside the shop to deter opportunistic cows.

" About 1965, one hot Saturday morning, Bearman's Department Store in High Road, Leytonstone, had all the doors open. A herd of cattle decided to come off the forest at the Green Man and came down the High Road, some going straight through the open doors and all hell broke out. As a young PC, I was called to help out and eventually a farmer from High Beech turned up and we drove the animals back onto the forest. This incident and others led to the placing of cattle grids where the Green Man and Waterworks Corner roundabouts are now.

FEAST AT THE FLORIST'S

Cows would especially take a liking to the flowers displayed outside florists' shops. They would eat as many flowers as they could before a shop assistant would run out waving a bunch of daffodils to shoo them away.

As a kid I loved going to Bearman's. I used to accompany my dad on a Saturday when he went to pay off the HP on our black and white telly. He would go to a little office at the top of the building while he left me to wallow in the toy department. To a young girl it seemed like the most ginormous department store in the whole world, when in reality it probably wasn't. It *was* reputedly the first store outside of London to have escalators, though.

All that inquisitiveness could sometimes lead a cow into a sticky situation. Reports of cows falling down steps or getting stuck in cattle grids abound:

" As a police cadet, I had to calm a cow who had fallen down a basement area in the front of a Victorian house in New Wanstead. We had to lift it out using a forklift tractor. "

And:

" I once remember a cow getting stuck in a grille at the entrance of Wanstead Cricket Club. The City of London police had to come and remove them. "

The more adventurous cows have been known to climb bridges. There used to be a pedestrian footbridge over Leytonstone High Road, linking Grove Road with Gainsborough Road – it had a sort of pram ramp up to it with very shallow, wide steps. One day a cow found its way onto the bridge and was too scared to get down again. Someone finally managed to coax it down onto the right side of the road and usher it back down towards Wanstead Flats. And legend has it that photographic evidence shows a cow on the old footbridge over Friday Hill in Chingford, but I'm still waiting for Dave to come up with the goods.

Cows are naturally curious animals and like to look in windows. Woe betide anyone who left their main windows open during the summertime. One lady remembers going into her front room to find a cow with its head stuck through the window eating from a vase of flowers.

HEY DIDDLE DIDDLE

One day a cow walked onto a bridge to have a good look at the traffic jam below.
The little dog in the car thought it was extremely funny.

Several people have mentioned being startled by cows sticking their heads in the windows of Whipps Cross Hospital:

> Cows used to wander into Whipps before the cattle grids were installed. It was a common occurrence for cows to stick their heads through the windows in the maternity unit - including the labour rooms whilst patients were giving birth. We often had to shoo them away out of the car park.

And:

> I woke up from an operation at Whipps Cross Hospital to be greeted with a big bullock's face plastered against the ward window.

Not the sort of thing you'd want to be confronted with if recovering from heart surgery. Though an unexpected appearance by a cow might have speeded up a difficult birth or brought a smile to the face of a poorly patient. After all, they do say laughter is the best medicine.

TEATIME TURMOIL

Mrs Dymchurch was having tea and cakes one afternoon when some cows looked in her dining room window. She dropped her romantic novel on the floor in surprise and spilled hot tea all over her stockings.

Several sports pitches in the area were part of the common land and were open to pedestrian access which also meant cows had a habit of wandering onto these areas, sometimes during the middle of an event, upsetting the play of the game and leaving deposits everywhere. A sticky situation, as a sliding tackle into a fresh cowpat was not uncommon for many a hapless footballer.

66 I used to organise various sports events, including inter-school football matches on Wanstead Flats. It was always quite interesting when the cows decided to make a pitch invasion during a game. What they left behind was of greater consequence and often had a big impact on the continuation of the game, especially when it was in the goal mouth. 99

If the resulting 'damage' to the pitch made it too hazardous to carry on, a retreat to the local pub was often the best compromise. But not before the embarrassment of being peered at by cows poking their heads round the doors of the sports changing room.

Woodford Golf Club, situated on the edge of the forest and unenclosed by fencing, was not immune to a visit by a few cows now and then. It wasn't too bad as long as they stayed in the rough, but once they ambled onto the greens it wasn't easy to get them off, particularly if you were down the other end of the fairway. Closer by, shouting and waving at them was not advisable. They might deem rowdy golfers a bit of an irritation and wander off in search of quieter pasture, but a grouchy cow bothered by being disturbed might just consider them fair play and charge. Suddenly, the open environment of a golf course would become very big indeed for a retreating golfer with no place to hide.

HOLED UP AT THE FOURTEENTH

Sometimes cows wandered onto the golf course next to the forest. Panic would break
out when they sat down on the putting greens. They liked the smooth surface, as it
was a perfect place for an afternoon snooze. But their big hooves made holes in the
green and they pooed everywhere. Mr Wood's golf ball landed 'SPLAT!' right on top
of a cowpat. Golfers would shout at the cows and wave their golf clubs in the air.

Greenkeepers would often have to pick up the pieces after a visitation by cows, especially when the ground was soft and thus churned up by cows' hooves. The head groundsman at Chingford Golf Club reputedly used to go 'absolutely potty if the cows got on to the golf course'. And a greenkeeper at the Woodford club remembers driving them off the greens on one occasion, only for them to return at night to 'continue their work' when no-one was looking.

Woodford Green Cricket Club, one of the oldest in the country, had similar tribulations of being invaded by cows. However, a team of cricketers may have had better fortune over a lone golfer at herding the cows off the pitch – or to 'cow corner' at the very least. Nevertheless, the club's scorebook allegedly has 'Cows Stop Play' written into it several times. The short grass of the pitch would have eventually caused the cows to seek out the lusher pasture of the adjoining common, but instead of waiting, all the players really needed to do was play the cows some music. Cows respond particularly well to being serenaded with a tune and they could easily have been led off the pitch in a Pied Piper fashion by someone playing a trombone or similar. A very good reason for all clubhouses to keep at least one musical instrument handy.

66 They used to come off the green and down our road. They even came in the garden. My dad brought a cow horn back from Switzerland and one day, he asked me to blow the horn loudly. Some cows suddenly appeared outside our house and I was convinced my cow horn had summoned them. 99

COWS STOP PLAY

One Sunday, during a game of cricket, some cows wandered onto the pitch to see what was going on. The game HAD to be stopped. Cricketers watched from the side of the pitch, tutting and huffing in annoyance as the cows wandered around the pitch, inspecting the stumps and leaving deposits everywhere. Mrs Tibbins the greengrocer's wife abandoned her picnic and ran screaming to the clubhouse when the cows went to sniff her sandwiches.

6. Where did all the cows go?

People continued to enjoy visitations by cows up until 1996. Every spring when the cows were turned out to pasture, hearts would be lifted at seeing these docile creatures wandering about, seemingly so out of place in a suburban landscape. A sense of continuity and familiarity could be felt at the cows returning for another year – for some it was a feeling of a connection with local customs still honoured, a rural idyll.

Or – hearts could be filled with doom at the prospect of another late morning into work, flowerbeds chomped, and the thought of scraping poo off your shoes.

So how come don't we see cows wandering about our streets anymore? What happened to the cows?

One spring morning in 1996, while grazing on Chingford Plain, the cows got carried off by some large and colourful kites. It was a particularly windy day and they flew off far, far away.

And that's how the cows disappeared from our landscape.

" I miss the cows. I've lived in Aldersbrook and Leytonstone and remember them visiting our roads all the time. Always in the garden eating the roses and taking up the whole pathway so you couldn't get in or out. We also had to dodge the pats on the way to school. It was lovely that they grazed on Wanstead Flats and could bring all cars to a standstill if they decided to cross Aldersbrook Road. "

KITE FLYING ON CHINGFORD PLAIN

Cows don't wander round the streets here anymore. Some people are quite pleased about this. The cows aren't around to cause traffic jams, or eat roses, or poo on pavements. They aren't around to interrupt cricket matches or spy in people's windows. Other people are sad, as the cows brought a little excitement into their daily lives and provided fertiliser and lawn mowing services. So what happened to the cows? One day, they went to eat grass on Chingford Plain, and got carried off by some kites. It was a particularly windy day and they flew off far, far away. Maybe they landed in a forest near you?

7. Value

The benefits that cows had brought to the landscape soon became evident when the quality of the grass began to deteriorate after cattle grazing ended. Shrubs and thickets became more prevalent, rank or coarse grass species increased while lower growing wildflower species decreased. Observations by local groups and individuals reported the loss or decline of some insects and butterflies.

Contrary to popular belief, cows do not eat just grass or grain; they are beasts of catholic tastes and will eat a wide variety of plants, given the chance. Herbs, tough plants, wild roses (*that's* where they got their taste for roses!) and brambles all contribute to making up a natural and healthy diet full of nutrients. They are even known to self-medicate when feeling unwell by eating willow leaves (willow, or salix, is the precursor of aspirin). Unlike sheep, which nibble and crop grass close to the ground, a cow will curl its tongue around a tuft of vegetation and pull it into its mouth. This action saves lower growing plants from being eaten while eliminating their tougher, more dominant competitors, keeping the common land from becoming a big overgrown thicket. Cows' hooves dig into the earth, breaking up the topsoil to form small depressions – ideal nurseries for wildflower seeds to settle and grow. These smaller wild plants are invaluable to other forms of life as food and sources of nectar. For example, certain species of butterflies will only use particular low-growing wildflowers as their foodplant for their caterpillars. Grazing helps in increasing the variety of different plants to thrive, which in turn attracts insects and invertebrates that feed off the plants and nectar, which in turn provide food for birds, bats and other small mammals and amphibians.

And of course there is the inevitable cow poo, which fertilises the soil, provides a growing medium for fungi and a meal for dung beetles and insect larvae, which in turn are eaten by birds…

…and so the cycle goes on.

TWENTY-FIRST-CENTURY FRONT GARDEN

It wasn't just cows that disappeared from our landscape. Front gardens have become an endangered species as people lose their primal connection with nature and convert them into car parks and dumping grounds for old furniture.

8. Cows today

"These cows have horns."

In a bid to improve the deteriorating grassland, a small herd of Longhorn cattle was introduced to Epping Forest at Fairmead in 2002 as part of a conservation project. They were tended by a herdsman until 2011, when a new type of corralling was introduced to keep the cows within designated areas and off the roads. Mindful of the Epping Forest Act and people's wishes for the forest to remain a truly open space without physical barriers, a revolutionary new 'invisible fencing' system was introduced.

It works like this. Where a normal fence would stand, a continuous wire is buried under the soil. This is linked electronically to a collar fitted round the cow's neck, and an audible warning noise is activated whenever the cow walks near the perimeter wire. The cow is trained to recognise this sound and walk no further; if it does, a mild shock is administered to the cow. Cows undergo a seven-day training period to get them used to the system before being 'let loose' into the forest. Now there are around 100 animals split into small groups grazing in the forest. They have developed into something of a novelty value – a tourist attraction, even – with their own page on the City of London's website and a link to a map showing where the cattle are currently grazing. They even received a visit from Prince Harry in 2017 when he visited the forest to view the Wood Pasture Restoration Project.

Early prototype of collar used in the location of invisible fencing.

LONGHORNS

After a while, people missed seeing the cows in the forest. Some farmers went out and bought some new ones, but everyone agreed that they shouldn't be allowed to wander round the streets anymore as they might cause an accident.

People didn't want the cows fenced off in the forest either, as people wouldn't be able to get inside the forest themselves.

So the farmers invented some 'invisible fencing' and trained their cows to wear a collar.

So you *can* still see cows wandering round the forest, it's just that they won't be able to come and eat the flowers in your front garden, or poo on the pavements any more.

9. The future?

The Epping Forest Wood Pasture Restoration Project was initiated in 2017 by the Queen's Commonwealth Canopy (QCC). It is an ambitious project to restore areas of ancient woodland through pollarding and grazing, thereby preserving Epping Forest's unique character. As a Site of Special Scientific Interest and a Special Area of Conservation, Epping Forest is one of only three QCC schemes in the UK and the whole of Europe, the majority (fifty-two) being situated in sub-equatorial areas of the world.

Future aims of the project include expanding the grazing herd to further improve the habitat and to re-engage with the lapsed 'commoners' (that's you and me) to encourage them to again graze livestock within the forest.

Got half an acre? Have a cow!

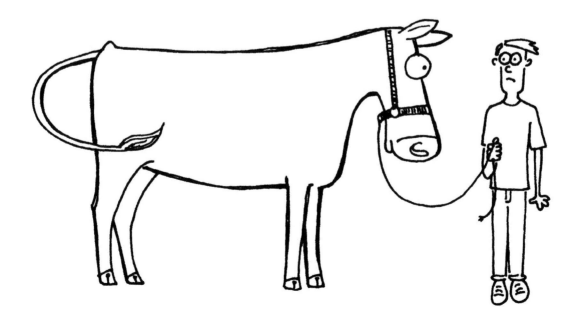

SANTA COWS

**** STOP PRESS ****

Remember those cows that got taken away by kites? Well, it is rumoured that a team of cows replaced Santa Claus's reindeer this year while they went off for a gap year in the tropics. Sightings of reindeer on a beach in Jamaica bear out this theory, as does the fact that this year's Christmas present delivery was rather haphazard.

10. A smidgeon of history

The history of Epping Forest, its rights of common and the Epping Forest Act are of great interest and worthy subjects for a book of their own. Indeed, I would recommend Sir William Addison's *Portrait of Epping Forest* to anyone wishing to explore this topic further. I won't attempt to write much more than the bare bones of the circumstances that led to cows remaining a feature of Epping Forest, as I'm not much of a historian. There are no doubt many local history enthusiasts who would all too gleefully trip me up into a fresh cowpat for something written in error.

Epping Forest was once part of a larger forest called the Forest of Waltham, which included Waltham Forest and Hainault Forest. For centuries, it has been a royal hunting forest – King Henry VIII built his medieval grandstand, or 'great standing', on the hill overlooking Chingford Plain in which to oversee the hunting of deer; we now know this building as the Queen Elizabeth Hunting Lodge. It was also a working forest – a place for commoners to graze livestock, and a source of timber for ships, construction and firewood. The bizarrely-shaped hornbeam, beech and oak trees you can see, especially around High Beach, are evidence of the continuous lopping (cutting) of branches at above head height (to prevent

roving deer and cattle eating the new growth). New shoots would sprout out from the cut-off point and a bulbous 'bole' would build up over the years. Nowadays, with the right of pollarding rescinded, growth goes unchecked and trees are in danger of getting top heavy. Therefore, specialist teams of tree surgeons have to move in to reduce the height of the trees.

Commons

Commons date back to medieval times and once covered half of the countryside in much of Britain. They were established when usage of them by local communities became enshrined as rights and recognised in law. Contrary to popular belief, common land is largely private land, held subject to certain privileges of use by the commoners. Each common's individual byelaws are different depending on the landscape and who owns the land, but some of the most common rights are:

- Right of pasturage – to graze sheep, cattle, horses, ponies, goats, geese, ducks.
- Right of estover – to pollard or coppice a tree, to take fallen timber for fuel or minor building work, or to take bracken for use as bedding.
- Right of pannage – to graze pigs on the 'mast' – fallen fruit of woodland trees (acorns, beechnuts, etc.) in autumn.
- Right of piscary – to take fish for personal consumption.

From the 1840s, as the population and urbanisation of the land around Epping Forest increased, the government turned a blind eye to the enclosure of land by the lords of the manor as it was viewed as being 'waste land'. And as royal hunting had declined, the Crown Lands and their rights were bought by the government for more profitable land development. In 1851, 3,000 acres of Hainault Forest were felled for arable farm use (the conurbations of modern-day Hainault and Barkingside now stand on what was a larger Hainault Forest). 4,000 acres of Epping Forest were illegally enclosed soon after. Many commoners lost their traditional rights or were evicted.

Commoners fought to save their way of life, and social and political reformers fought to preserve the forest and keep it open for the public's recreation. The newly-formed Commons Preservation Society (early members included John Stuart Mill, William Morris, Sir Robert Hunter and Octavia Hill – the last two founding the National Trust in 1895) – invited The Corporation of London (now The City of London Corporation) in to help. The Corporation used its influence to stop the enclosures with a lawsuit based on the rights of intercommonage – the right to graze animals over adjoining commons. As the City of London Cemetery is based within the forest at Aldersbrook, its owner – the Corporation of London – could be technically classed as a commoner. As a result, in 1874, the enclosures were declared illegal. The Corporation bought out the ownership of the land from the government and lords of the manor, and compensation was paid to those who would necessarily lose some rights of common through modifications needed to preserve the forest and its habitat. Lopping Hall in Loughton was built in compensation for the community's lost lopping rights.

In 1878, the Epping Forest Act was passed, establishing the City of London as the Conservators of Epping Forest. This act laid down a stipulation that the Conservators:

> ...shall at all times keep Epping Forest unenclosed and unbuilt on as an open space for the recreation and enjoyment of the people.

Most rights of common over the forest were removed, apart from the rights of pasturage and pannage which were retained and protected. Any resident within a forest parish who had half an acre of land was allowed to graze cattle on the common land at a rate of four pounds per two cattle per annum.

The forest was formally opened in a great fanfare by Queen Victoria at High Beach on 6th May 1882.

In the latter half of the twentieth century, as the land around the forest became steadily more urbanised and the quantity of motor vehicles increased, there were intermittent calls for grazing to be stopped because of the danger to/from traffic and people. But despite debates in local newspapers and some colourful banter in the House of Lords, grazing continued, even though an ever-dwindling number of commoners took advantage of their grazing rights. However, an amendment was made to the Epping Forest Act in 1977 to restrict the grazing rights to between 15th April until 15th November, primarily to prevent run-ins between cows and cars during the darkness of the winter rush-hours.

Soon though, there were clouds on the horizon. In the 1980s, a new fatal disease in cattle – bovine spongiform encephalopathy (BSE), or 'mad cow disease' – was diagnosed.

Then in 1996, it was discovered that it was transmittable to humans in the form of Creutzfeldt-Jakob disease (CJD). In order to eliminate the disease from the UK, the government ordered the culling of all cattle over the age of thirty months. Sadly there were no kites flying that day for those cows.

Happily, in 2002, grazing was re-established as part of a conservation project. A small herd of Longhorn cattle were grazed at Fairmead and Chingford Plain, supervised by a herdsman to keep them within the designated areas. After successful trials of the invisible fencing system, cattle can now be seen grazing over a wider area of the forest. You can just see the electronic collar hanging round the cow's neck (above).

Cows elsewhere

Cows on commons aren't just a peculiarity to Epping Forest. There are 7,000 commons in England, ranging in size from national parks, such as the Lake District and the New Forest, right down to areas of less than a hectare. Of these, some 1,400 have rights to graze cattle registered on them.

Cambridge is perhaps the best-known town where cattle can still be seen on the commons. Some 120 cows graze on the parks and grassland within sight of the university in an idyllic pastoral setting, where they do an excellent job of lawnmowing. They are much-loved by the Cantabrigians for the impression it gives them of rusticity in town, or of being in the countryside.

Minchinhampton and Rodborough Commons near Stroud in Gloucestershire are two more well-known and adjoining commons occupied by cows. Up to 500 cows are turned out each spring for marking day on 13th May. Grazing is an essential part of managing the commons to keep the rich diversity of wildlife species flourishing there.

Walton Common in Somerset has recently had the invisible fencing system installed. A small herd of miniature Dexter cows – which are not much bigger than Shetland ponies – have been released to improve the grassland and preserve the visibility of the area's Iron Age settlement.

Burnham Beeches in Buckinghamshire is another site under the stewardship of the City of London Corporation. This forest has a similar history of usage to Epping Forest, and was bought by the Corporation in 1880 to protect it from enclosure and development. Here Exmoor ponies and pigs graze alongside British White cattle, again using electronic collars to keep them within safe boundaries.

And in London, the grazing of sheep and cows was trialled in Green Park for a short period in 2018, with a view to expanding it further in the future, while a small herd of Belted Galloway cows is a permanent fixture in Richmond Park.

So who knows? With the small but growing shift towards pasture fed, higher welfare beef, small scale cattle grazing may become a more familiar sight across the country as authorities move to a gentler, more holistic way of managing the vegetation of our green open spaces, and a more natural, kinder and healthier way of raising cattle.

Afterword:
Adventures in paper making

Some time after I'd created my cow paintings, I began to wonder how I could establish links with my art and the cows that now graze certain parts of Epping Forest. With an art exhibition at Lopping Hall looming fast on the horizon (there's one link for a start – see previous chapter), it's always a canny idea to have a deeper connection with your subject matter. Makes it look like you know what you're talking about.

Anyhoo, I remembered seeing Ellie Poo paper in the Atlantis Art shop a few years back and it got me thinking. If some bright spark had had the idea to make paper out of elephant dung, maybe they, or another manufacturer, had done the same with cow dung? I consulted the oracle Google for such a supplier, but none were forthcoming, apart from a company in the USA who made 'poopoo' jotters. Too small for my purposes, and not chunky enough, if you know what I mean.

However, there did seem to be quite a bit of interest in using cow poo for all sorts of other products. The indigenous peoples of many regions in Africa and Asia have been using it as a traditional building material for centuries. Hindus use dried cow dung as fuel and in products such as soaps and medicines, based on tried and trusted formulas from ancient Ayurvedic texts. Drinking cow's urine – *gau mutra* – is considered beneficial, and various soft drinks are marketed as a healthy alternative to cola (Cow-ca Cola, anyone?). Indeed, it seems you can shop for just about anything in certain regions of India and it will contain one or other waste products from the sacred cow.

Aside from India, it seems there are many ventures popping up in various parts of the world looking at the versatile product that is cow dung. Countries are investing in its use as a biofuel, and it is widely used as a building material, as an insect repellent and in composts and fertilisers. While on a more local level, enterprising young sorts are making fabrics and furniture out of faeces.

Back to my search for cow poo paper, which wasn't going well. I had to face it. If I wanted to get myself an alternative drawing medium there was only one thing for it. I would have to make it myself.

How does one make paper? I'm quite a creative sort, but papermaking was not something I'd ever tried. I had a vague idea that its actions had similarities to panning for gold, but I really needed to read up on the techniques, ratios of ingredients and so on. I bought a book on the subject and duly made, according to the instructions, a frame out of an old net curtain stretched over an old picture frame in readiness for the making of paper.

Now I needed some paper pulp. No problem with that, I have plenty of spare paper, and the required PVA glue too. Cow poo. Where do I get cow poo?

I considered buying cow dung on Amazon – they sell it conveniently as dried 'cakes' to be used as fuel. But then that wouldn't have any special link with 'our' cows and would defeat the object of the exercise. Similarly, dried cow poo powder would be meaningless. There was only one thing for it. An expedition to Chingford Plain was required, to locate and bring back a quantity of cow poo from the indigenous Longhorns of Epping Forest.

Armed with a bucket, rubber gloves, a trowel, clingfilm and some plastic bags, I set off on probably the hottest day in June in search of poo. I must just mention here that I don't drive, so I took off for Chingford on the bus.

Well, it wasn't hard to locate what I was looking for. There were dollops of it everywhere. In every stage, from fresh creamy plops to dried frisbees. Bending down, scooping some of the squishier stuff into my bucket, I looked up to see a group of cows slowly ambling towards me, cropping the grass as they went.

What a magnificent sight! And my word, aren't they big! Much bigger than the black and white Friesians that used to wander the streets years ago. These ones look twice as big and bulky, and are armed with a fearsome set of horns to boot. Their colouration is a pleasing mix of shades of brown interlaced with white – what we called 'roan' in horsey circles, or brindle, with streaks of black running through the brown. They strolled towards me as a group, tails languidly swishing in the midday sun. They would occasionally raise their heads to locate a juicier patch of grass or wander off into the longer scrub if families out for a Sunday walk got too close or made too much noise. I kept a safe distance away as they sauntered slowly past, but on one occasion when I had my camera up to my face I was transfixed with a penetrating stare from one of the cows. Our eyes met. Ears pricked. For one heart-stopping moment I was sure this particular cow was going to head over in my direction, bringing her chums with her to find out what the hell I was doing staring at her with that large black cyclops. Animals seem to have an aversion to cameras – maybe

they, like the native American Indians, believe them to be soul-stealers. But she didn't. She slowly lowered her head to the ground and resumed her business eating grass. I watched them for some time after as they made their way into the thickets and carried on scooping poop into my bucket.

I had collected near enough a whole bucket full of dung and estimated this amount should be ample for my needs. Besides, it was jolly heavy, and I had a long walk back to the bus stop in the sweltering heat. I wrapped the top of the bucket in clingfilm and put the whole thing in a large plastic bag. I had to appear as if I'd been Sunday shopping at the local supermarket and was laden down with potatoes and other heavy items so as not to raise suspicion from the bus driver.

Well, the bus driver either didn't notice or was too bored to mention my cumbersome cargo, and I safely smuggled it to the back of the bus where I had ample room to place it between my feet. I don't know whether it was the heat of the day or the fact that I was sitting over the boiling, chugging bus engine, but the heat began to rise and so too did the smell. Fortunately, there were not many passengers that day and if they did catch a whiff, I'd have to pretend I'd trodden in a cowpat or had an accident in my underpants. Thankfully, I think they all had hayfever or were too polite to mention the smell, which wasn't too bad, really.

Back home I unwrapped my bucket on the lawn in the back garden. My husband John and his pal Paul, lazing on easy chairs on the patio, ice cold drinks in hand, regarded me with amusement, wondering what I'd do next.

So here's how I did it. You can join in if you like. A word of caution – I'm not very good at following recipes and just tend to make things up as I go along, which is probably why I have so many disasters. If you wish to have a go yourself, I would strongly recommend getting a book on papermaking and familiarise yourself with the techniques. Properly.

- In small batches, rinse the poo several times, separating the plant fibres from the liquid with a sieve. Squeezing out the liquid speeds up the process a bit, and the diluted poo liquid goes straight on the flower beds. It is advisable to wear rubber gloves.

- Once the water is more or less clear, it is ready for making into paper. You can do this straight away or leave it to dry out, to be reconstituted later.

- Here you can see the plant fibres dried out. The smell is minimal, like dried grass and not at all poo-ey. Looks a bit like Weetabix, doesn't it?

- Prepare your paper pulp. Tear or shred some plain white paper and soak it in water. If you shred it small, it will take less time to be rendered into a mush. Put the mush in a large tray, big enough to take your netted frame. Add water, some PVA glue and the cow poo plant fibres. It's advisable to reconstitute dried fibres first in a smaller bowl of water, otherwise you'll have little dried lumps bobbing about on the surface like granola.

- When it's all thoroughly mixed and the consistency of thin porridge, submerge the netted frame into the mixture. Swill it about a bit, lift it out, and with any luck the mixture will have arranged itself evenly over the frame, and the liquid will drain back into the bath.

- Getting the pulp from the frame onto a drying rack is a feat in itself. There's a technique for flipping the paper in one swift wrist action that I mastered after a fashion, but not until after much cursing, swearing and screwed-up blobs of disintegrated paper pulp. You can leave the paper to dry in the sun as I did or stack it between kitchen cloths and newspaper to dry out more slowly.

Here are the finished results. The paper is quite fragile, light grey in colour, with a pleasing rusticity about it. Plant fibres are visible, along with the odd bit of beetle carapace from an unfortunate dung beetle caught in the mix. In trialling materials on the paper, I found watercolours disintegrated the paper somewhat – maybe I needed to use more PVA in the mixture. Acrylic paints worked well with a minimum of water. In this medium I painted eight of the dinky little 'cowtoons' shown here for the exhibition. I used a charcoal drawing pencil on the head sketch, but had to proceed carefully as the pencil was liable to snag larger fibres and cause the paper to rip.

All in all, a fruitful exercise, and one that I will be repeating again. Just don't tell the bus driver.

The End

Thank you

Everyone who contributed to the crowdfunding for this book. Production wouldn't have been possible without all you lovely people.

Thank you to:

Louise Baker
Christine Brassey
Mary Cavanagh
Sue Day
Sue & Mick Dunn
Colin Raymond Dyer-Jones
Nick & Martine Elliott
Kate Gloudemans
Melanie Hall
Sara Hennessy
Elin Henty
Sue Jay
Angela & Graham Kane
Anthony Khan
Peter Lawrence
Donna Lennon & Paul Furlong

Tricia Moxey
Kay O'Grady
Kian & Aiden O'Grady
Martyn Partridge
Julie Pearce
Diane Rhodes
Rowley Gallery
Louise Sargeant
Alex Stutchbury
Bernie Tynan
David Varney
John Wagstaff
Kathryn Webb
June White
Andrew Wright
Margaret Wyatt

Special thanks to:

Alex Stutchbury, Mary Cavanagh and Melanie Hall for critical discussion and encouragement.

The Rowley Gallery for framing, and The Lopping Hall Gallery for exhibiting.

Year 3 pupils at St John's Primary School in Buckhurst Hill – for giving my paintings such a wonderful reception, and for all your smashing drawings of cows.

To Kai Lam – for suggesting I put all my paintings in a book in the first place.

To my long-suffering husband John, who has endured many lonesome nights while I have been painting and tappity-tapping away on the computer in the study. And to Widgie the cat, for keeping my lap warm and reminding me when it's time to stop.

Acknowledgements

Thank you to all those who contributed to my posts on Facebook through groups: Remembering Woodford Green, Epping Forest Forum and Wanstead Community Hub. Your anecdotes have provided me with a wealth of inspiration, firstly in my paintings and secondly in the writing of this book. In particular:

Frontispiece

Inspiration: Christine Brassey (Cow with Purpose)

Chapter 1: How it all began

Quote: Karen Marcelle Cowan

Chapter 2: Gardens

Quotes: Emma Buckley, Gus Fletcher
Photos: Adrian & Maralyn Ryan, Stephen Tant, Connie Fletcher
Inspiration: Stephen Tant (Mayhem in Monkhams)

Chapter 3: Traffic

Quotes: Sue Nelson, Claire Rumble, Dr Julian Litten, Pat Cutler, Christine Brassey, Peter Lawrence
Photos: Irene and John Buchan, E7NowandThen, Graham Frankel
Inspiration: Julian Litten (Encounter at the Crossing)

Chapter 4: Cowpats

Quotes: Vick Routh, David Bambridge, Daisy Russell, Sue Jay, Mark Anthony C Davis, Maxine Cohen
Photos: Peter Haseldine, Anon
Inspiration: David Bambridge (Moonlight Encounter)

Chapter 5: Inquisitiveness

Quotes: Peter Lawrence, Scott Wilding, Anon, Roger Matthews, Steve Chandler, Hilary Jayne Matthews
Photos: Roger Godbold, Jill Stock, Graham Frankel, Stephen Jackson
Inspiration: Michele Gascoine (Buds), Jan Raynes (Hey Diddle Diddle), Maxine Cohen (Exotic Pets), Norma Barry (Cows Stop Play)
https://www.guardian-series.co.uk/news/localhistory/10112446.bearmans-department-store-remembered/

Chapter 6: Where did all the cows go?

Quotes: Louise Russell

Chapter 7: Value

The importance of grazing for wildlife conservation, PDF, publications.naturalengland.org.uk/file/612038
https://butterfly-conservation.org/
www.wansteadwildlife.org.uk
www.pastureforlife.org
The Secret Life of Cows – Rosamund Young

Chapter 8: Cows today

https://www.cityoflondon.gov.uk/things-to-do/green-spaces/epping-forest/wildlife-and-nature/Pages/cattle-grazing.aspx

https://www.longhorncattlesociety.com/

https://api.parliament.uk/historic-hansard/lords/1968/nov/05/epping-forest-cattle-grazing

Invisible Fencing for Conservation Grazing: a user's guide:

https://www.youtube.com/watch?v=kxz7nR17WE8

http://www.foundationforcommonland.org.uk/

https://www.bbc.co.uk/news/uk-45906585

Chapter 9: The Future?

https://queenscommonwealthcanopy.org/projects/epping-forest/

Chapter 10: A smidgeon of history

Photos: Karen Humpage, Adrian and Maralyn Ryan, David Horlick

Apologies to local historians

Portrait of Epping Forest – Sir William Addison

https://www.cityoflondon.gov.uk/things-to-do/green-spaces/epping-forest/heritage/Pages/history-of-Epping-Forest.aspx

https://www.oss.org.uk/who-we-are/about-us/ – Commons Preservation Society

http://www.foundationforcommonland.org.uk/rights-of-common

Klaudia Baker – The Warren (Corporation of London)

https://www.midsummercommon.org.uk/Grazing/page.html

https://www.independent.co.uk/environment/cambridge-cattle-cows-commons-why-parks-livestock-countryside-urbanisation-a8460171.html

https://www.nationaltrust.org.uk/minchinhampton-and-rodborough-commons/features/for-the-common-good

https://www.avonwildlifetrust.org.uk/news/2016/07/07/dexter-cattle-help-restore-our-reserve

https://www.royalparks.org.uk/

Afterword: Adventures in paper making

http://www.bcu.ac.uk/news-events/news/your-furniture-is-poo-student-transforms-cow-manure-into-household-furniture

http://jalilaessaidi.com/cowmanure/

https://www.globalcitizen.org/en/content/who-uses-sht-to-build-a-house/

https://www.telegraph.co.uk/expat/expatnews/7398029/Cow-dung-and-urine-healthy.html

https://www.theguardian.com/world/2018/aug/01/the-start-up-making-shirts-out-of-cow-poo

https://fashionunited.uk/news/fashion/dutch-designer-makes-fashion-out-of-cow-dung/2016083021576

https://www.bbc.co.uk/programmes/articles/X9VfhMW6P2p2qp3hQJVQb3/nine-brilliant-ideas-for-recycling-waste

Further Reading

Wilding – Isabella Tree

Portrait of Epping Forest – Sir William Addison

The Secret Life of Cows – Rosamund Young

Trees in the Wild – Gerald Wilkinson

The importance of grazing for wildlife conservation, PDF, publications.naturalengland.org.uk/file/612038

pastureforlife.org

wansteadwildlife.org.uk

https://www.cityoflondon.gov.uk/things-to-do/green-spaces/epping-forest/about-us/Documents/1878-Epping-Forest-Act.pdf – The Epping Forest Act